D1535999

All About Food Crops

WHEAT

Cecelia H. Brannon

Enslow Publishing
101 W. 23rd Street
Suite 240
New York, NY 10011
USA

enslow.com

Published in 2018 by Enslow Publishing, LLC
101 W. 23rd Street, Suite 240 New York, NY 10011

Library of Congress Cataloging-in-Publication Data

Names: Brannon, Cecelia H., author. | Brannon, Cecelia H. All about food crops.
Title: Wheat / Cecelia H. Brannon.
Description: New York, NY : Enslow Publishing, 2018. | Series: All about food crops | Audience: Pre-K to grade 1. | Includes bibliographical references and index.
Identifiers: LCCN 2017002025| ISBN 9780766085855 (library-bound) | ISBN 9780766088252 (pbk.) | ISBN 9780766088191 (6-pack)
Subjects: LCSH: Wheat—Juvenile literature.
Classification: LCC SB191.W5 B73 2018 | DDC 633.1/1—dc23
LC record available at https://lccn.loc.gov/2017002025

Printed in the United States of America

To Our Readers: We have done our best to make sure all websites in this book were active and appropriate when we went to press. However, the author and the publisher have no control over and assume no liability for the material available on those websites or on any websites they may link to. Any comments or suggestions can be sent by email to customerservice@enslow.com.

Photo Credits: Cover, p. 1 YuriyZhuravov/Shutterstock.com; pp. 3 (left), 18 Vitezslav Halamka/Shutterstock.com; pp. 3 (center), 14 Gayvoronskaya_Yana/Shutterstock.com; pp. 3 (right), 12 Daria Grebenchuk/Shutterstock.com; pp. 4–5 5 second Studio/Shutterstock.com; p. 6 Marco Ossino/Shutterstock.com; p. 8 Andreja Donko/Shutterstock.com; p. 10 The Vine Studios/Shutterstock.com; p. 16 Doro Guzenda/Shutterstock.com; p. 20 Scorpp/Shutterstock.com; p. 22 wavebreakmedia/Shutterstock.com.

Contents

Words to Know

bushel   kernels   straw

Wheat is an important crop.

Wheat grows in a large field. Kansas grows the most wheat in the United States.

Wheat grows green, but it is not ready to be picked until it turns brown.

Wheat is a type of grass. The stalks can grow to be seven feet (two meters) tall!

The dry stalks are called straw. Straw is used to make hats and baskets.

Wheat has seeds called kernels. Sometimes kernels are called wheat berries.

The wheat kernels are ground up to make flour.

One bushel of wheat makes about 42 pounds (19 kilograms) of flour.

Flour is used to make bread, pasta, pizza dough, cakes, pies, cookies, bagels, cereal, crackers, and so much more!

Many people eat wheat
every day.

Read More

Hayes, Amy. *Turning Wheat into Bread*. New York, NY: Cavendish Square Publishing, 2015.

Owen, Ruth. *Bread! Life on a Wheat Farm*. New York, NY: Windmill Books, 2012.

Rattini, Kristin Baird. *National Geographic Readers: Seed to Plant*. Washington, DC: National Geographic, 2014.

Websites

Kids Cooking Activities
www.kids-cooking-activities.com/grain-facts.html
Learn more about wheat and other grains and check out a tasty bread recipe to try with an adult!

National Association of Wheat Growers
www.wheatworld.org/wheat-101/wheat-facts/
Read more facts about wheat.

Index

Guided Reading Level: B
Guided Reading Leveling System is based on the guidelines recommended by Fountas and Pinnell.

Word Count: 121